SPOTLIGHT ON
AN EQUITABLE WORLD

SOCIAL CHANGE

Mary Ratzer

ROSEN
PUBLISHING

Published in 2025 by The Rosen Publishing Group, Inc.
2544 Clinton Street, Buffalo, NY 14224

First Edition

Editor: Greg Roza
Book Design: Michael Flynn

Photo Credits: Cover Hero Images Inc/Shutterstock.com; cover, p. 3 (hands) Dedraw Studio/Shutterstock.com; (series Earth icon) v4ndhira/Shutterstock.com; p. 5 UPI / Alamy Stock Photo; p. 6 Veja/Shutterstock.com; p. 7 Susan C. Brown/Shutterstock.com; p. 9 mavo/Shutterstock.com; p. 10 Halfpoint/Shutterstock.com; p. 11 SeventyFour/Shutterstock.com; p. 13 https://commons.wikimedia.org/wiki/File:The_universal_declaration_of_human_rights_10_December_1948.jpg; p. 14 Mega Pixel/Shutterstock.com; p. 15 Sergey Novikov/Shutterstock.com; p. 17 Africa Studio/Shutterstock.com; p. 18 Andrey_Popov/Shutterstock.com; p. 19 Sheila Fitzgerald/Shutterstock.com; p. 21 SB Arts Media/Shutterstock.com; p. 22 Prostock-studio/Shutterstock.com; p. 23 Roy Harris/Shutterstock.com; p. 25 Dragana Gordic/Shutterstock.com; p. 26 bleakstar/Shutterstock.com; p. 27 SpeedKingz/Shutterstock.com; p. 29 Pixel-Shot/Shutterstock.com.

Cataloging-in-Publication Data

Names: Ratzer, Mary Boyd.
Title: Social change / Mary Ratzer.
Description: Buffalo, NY : Rosen Young Adult, 2025. | Series: Spotlight on an equitable world | Includes glossary and index.
Identifiers: ISBN 9781499477412 (pbk.) | ISBN 9781499477238 (library bound) | ISBN 9781499476958 (ebook)
Subjects: LCSH: Social change--Juvenile literature. | Social action--Juvenile literature.
Classification: LCC HM831.R38 2025 | DDC 303.4--dc23

Manufactured in the United States of America

CPSIA Compliance Information: Batch #CSRYA25. For further information contact Rosen Publishing at 1-800-237-9932.

CONTENTS

Chapter One

SOCIAL CHANGE AND VALUES

Many young people have been inspired to act when they see the need for change in their world. They have strong values regarding inequality in society based on race, gender, and other things. They respond by taking action. Many people just like you have taken opportunities to be a part of solving problems. They've become voices for change for many issues, including climate change, gun violence, and racism. You have an open door to active citizenship waiting for you. Be aware of your own power to step up and make a difference!

Many young citizens use different parts of their lives (as consumers, workers, and community members) to influence change. You can keep the social impact and social responsibility in mind when purchasing goods or exploring the job market. Many people who value community and social justice choose to support socially responsible companies. Do you ask yourself if products you want to buy are sustainable for the planet? Do you feel good about buying from a company that demonstrates that it's socially responsible? Companies too can use their values to work for social change.

Many young people want to work for companies where they can be a part of making a difference for their community. This sense of purpose affects their decisions on jobs. Corporate social responsibility is increasingly creating social change and workforce decisions. Active citizenship has made a strong impact on job searches, worker morale, and company loyalty.

In 2014, when they were 8 and 6 years old, brothers Brandon and Sebastian Martinez founded Are You Kidding Socks. The company works with and draws attention to numerous charities.

Chapter Two

EMPATHY NOT APATHY

Sometimes people go through days occupied only with their activities and connections with friends. Will they even notice if someone is knocked down in the hallway at school or bullied on the bus? If you have empathy, it can motivate you to be an ally and give people in need your support. On the other hand, apathy, or a lack of caring, can keep you from seeing problems around you. Some call this "happy apathy," because you just enjoy your daily routine instead of seeing issues. Seeing people in bad situations—including homeless people, children without proper clothes in winter, or parents who cannot feed their family—can be unsettling. However, some people would rather ignore these situations rather than care about them. When you see unfairness, can you choose empathy instead of apathy?

Habitat for Humanity is an organization that builds affordable homes for those who need them. Volunteers help build or repair the homes.

Seeing social injustice in your world can connect you with your community. But awareness also can cause anxiety. Perhaps you feel powerless or overwhelmed. You might think that you can't make a positive effect. But recognizing injustice can start the process of finding a way to help. This can involve investigating, talking to trusted adults, and finding allies who might join you. Empathy can keep you from giving up.

One real-world example is a high school student who has dedicated herself to helping others. She created a way to help other kids who need a buddy system to play sports. The organization pairs kids with disabilities with buddies, creating unified sports teams that can compete, connect, and have fun. This active citizen also works for Habitat for Humanity, helping to build homes for people in need.

Chapter Three

STUDENTS START WITH A PROBLEM

Active citizens ready to work for social change identify issues important to their lives and community. Students in a global issues class in Aurora, Colorado, decided to support refugees in their town. They addressed barriers that many immigrants face in launching their own businesses. The students had learned how to start a business, make a business plan, and manage finances, so they had useful background knowledge to bring to the project.

One student in the class had lived in the Democratic Republic of the Congo and came to America as a refugee herself. She wanted to run a small business and cared about the future of the local refugee population. She and her peers researched ways that the state of Colorado supported refugees. Their plan to support refugees in start-up businesses went beyond programs already available in the state. Students went to the state legislature and shared their plan for supporting refugees seeking a better future.

Their solution used funding from state taxes to create a space where refugee start-up businesses could grow. The students proposed rent-free space to work, education on how to start and run a business, and interest-free loans. Leaders put together a draft bill. These active student citizens showed that the talent and creativity of refugees can enrich their community.

Small business owners can flourish when they are supported by citizens and leaders of the community. This in turn helps the community grow stronger.

Chapter Four

HALL OF FAME

Suppose there is a Justice for All Hall of Fame honoring those who are making the world a better place. Let's take a tour of those recognized in the Hall of Fame.

- **One group of college soccer players organized and coached a team of refugee boys. The kids formed friendships and had fun with a sport they all knew and loved.**
- **In the wake of tornado destruction in Texas, some high school football teams organized cleanup for the affected communities.**
- **Restaurants in many cities have organized a way to package and share leftover food at the end of the day instead of throwing it out.**
- **Families from a local mosque worked to support refugees who fled violence in Afghanistan. They found them homes, jobs, English classes, clothes, food, and a welcoming community.**

Volunteering at a local soup kitchen is a good way to start participating in social change.

- Some farms provide free community gardens for people without access to fresh fruits and vegetables.
- An action group worked to raise funds and restore a community swimming pool in a low-income area.
- In some areas, after-school programs for kids have expanded to provide volunteer homework help and dinner.
- Some high school students tutored senior citizens in the use of computers and tablets at senior centers.
- A soup kitchen serves lunch every day for over 100 homeless people, using donations from gardeners, grocery stores, and a food pantry.
- Local volunteers provide support for veterans suffering from trauma and stress by pairing them with therapy horses.
- Volunteers help provide summer camp experiences for kids from New York City.

Chapter Five

RESOURCES, OPPORTUNITIES, AND RIGHTS

The United Nations works for global social justice. The UN tracks unfairness and injustice and tries to solve problems by providing people with resources and opportunities. Social change is part of its purpose. UN evidence shows a world of haves and have-nots. However, many people work every day to try to bring fairness to an unfair world.

The evidence defines the action that is needed to solve the problems around the world:

- **Income and the opportunity to earn money** from work varies widely. While some billionaires live in mansions and own airplanes, the minimum wage in many U.S. states is only $7.25, making it difficult for many Americans to make a living.
- **The opportunity to own property,** especially a home, is affected by income. Upper-income earners have a huge advantage. A lower income and the lack of availability of low-cost housing are huge disadvantages.
- **Opportunities for good-paying jobs** are mostly available to those who've been able to access (and pay for) higher educational opportunities. Those who've only graduated from high school may struggle for a living wage. Many people, even with college experience and degrees, may need to work more than one job to pay for rent and groceries.

THE UNIVERSAL DECLARATION OF Human Rights

WHEREAS *recognition of the inherent dignity and of the equal and inalienable rights of all members of the human family is the foundation of freedom, justice and peace in the world,*

WHEREAS *disregard and contempt for human rights have resulted in barbarous acts which have outraged the conscience of mankind, and the advent of a world in which human beings shall enjoy freedom of speech and belief and freedom from fear and want has been proclaimed as the highest aspiration of the common people,*

WHEREAS *it is essential, if man is not to be compelled to have recourse, as a last resort, to rebellion against tyranny and oppression, that human rights should be protected by the rule of law,*

WHEREAS *it is essential to promote the development of friendly relations among nations,*

WHEREAS *the peoples of the United Nations have in the Charter reaffirmed their faith in fundamental human rights, in the dignity and worth of the human person and in the equal rights of men and women and have determined to promote social progress and better standards of life in larger freedom,*

WHEREAS *Member States have pledged themselves to achieve, in co-operation with the United Nations, the promotion of universal respect for and observance of human rights and fundamental freedoms,*

WHEREAS *a common understanding of these rights and freedoms is of the greatest importance for the full realisation of this pledge,*

NOW THEREFORE THE GENERAL ASSEMBLY

PROCLAIMS *this Universal Declaration of Human Rights as a common standard of achievement for all peoples and all nations, to the end that every individual and every organ of society, keeping this Declaration constantly in mind, shall strive by teaching and education to promote respect for these rights and freedoms and by progressive measures, national and international, to secure their universal and effective recognition and observance, both among the peoples of Member States themselves and among the peoples of territories under their jurisdiction.*

ARTICLE 1 —All human beings are born free and equal in dignity and rights. They are endowed with reason and conscience and should act towards one another in a spirit of brotherhood.

ARTICLE 2 —1. Everyone is entitled to all the rights and freedoms set forth in this Declaration, without distinction of any kind, such as race, colour, sex, language, religion, political or other opinion, national or social origin, property, birth or other status.
2. Furthermore, no distinction shall be made on the basis of the political, jurisdictional or international status of the country or territory to which a person belongs, whether this territory be an independent, Trust or Non-Self-Governing territory, or under any other limitation of sovereignty.

ARTICLE 3 —Everyone has the right to life, liberty and the security of person.

ARTICLE 4 —No one shall be held in slavery or servitude; slavery and the slave trade shall be prohibited in all their forms.

ARTICLE 5 —No one shall be subjected to torture or to cruel, inhuman or degrading treatment or punishment.

ARTICLE 6 —Everyone has the right to recognition everywhere as a person before the law.

ARTICLE 7 —All are equal before the law and are entitled without any discrimination to equal protection of the law. All are entitled to equal protection against any discrimination in violation of this Declaration and against any incitement to such discrimination.

ARTICLE 8 —Everyone has the right to an effective remedy by the competent national tribunals for acts violating the fundamental rights granted him by the constitution or by law.

ARTICLE 9 —No one shall be subjected to arbitrary arrest, detention or exile.

ARTICLE 10 —Everyone is entitled in full equality to a fair and public hearing by an independent and impartial tribunal, in the determination of his rights and obligations and of any criminal charge against him.

ARTICLE 11 —1. Everyone charged with a penal offence has the right to be presumed innocent until proved guilty according to law in a public trial at which he has had all the guarantees necessary for his defence.
2. No one shall be held guilty of any penal offence on account of any act or omission which did not constitute a penal offence, under national or international law, at the time when it was committed. Nor shall a heavier penalty be imposed than the one that was applicable at the time the penal offence was committed.

ARTICLE 12 —No one shall be subjected to arbitrary interference with his privacy, family, home or correspondence, nor to attacks upon his honour and reputation. Everyone has the right to the protection of the law against such interference or attacks.

ARTICLE 13 —1. Everyone has the right to freedom of movement and residence within the borders of each state.
2. Everyone has the right to leave any country, including his own, and to return to his country.

ARTICLE 14 —1. Everyone has the right to seek and to enjoy in other countries asylum from persecution.
2. This right may not be invoked in the case of prosecutions genuinely arising from non-political crimes or from acts contrary to the purposes and principles of the United Nations.

ARTICLE 15 —1. Everyone has the right to a nationality.
2. No one shall be arbitrarily deprived of his nationality nor denied the right to change his nationality.

ARTICLE 16 —1. Men and women of full age, without any limitation due to race, nationality or religion, have the right to marry and to found a family. They are entitled to equal rights as to marriage, during marriage and at its dissolution.
2. Marriage shall be entered into only with the free and full consent of the intending spouses.
3. The family is the natural and fundamental group unit of society and is entitled to protection by society and the State.

ARTICLE 17 —1. Everyone has the right to own property alone as well as in association with others.
2. No one shall be arbitrarily deprived of his property.

ARTICLE 18 —Everyone has the right to freedom of thought, conscience and religion; this right includes freedom to change his religion or belief, and freedom, either alone or in community with others and in public or private, to manifest his religion or belief in teaching, practice, worship and observance.

ARTICLE 19 —Everyone has the right to freedom of opinion and expression; this right includes freedom to hold opinions without interference and to seek, receive and impart information and ideas through any media and regardless of frontiers.

ARTICLE 20 —1. Everyone has the right to freedom of peaceful assembly and association.
2. No one may be compelled to belong to an association.

ARTICLE 21 —1. Everyone has the right to take part in the government of his country, directly or through freely chosen representatives.
2. Everyone has the right of equal access to public service in his country.
3. The will of the people shall be the basis of the authority of government; this will shall be expressed in periodic and genuine elections which shall be by universal and equal suffrage and shall be held by secret vote or by equivalent free voting procedures.

ARTICLE 22 —Everyone, as a member of society, has the right to social security and is entitled to realisation, through national effort and international co-operation and in accordance with the organisation and resources of each State, of the economic, social and cultural rights indispensable for his dignity and the free development of his personality.

ARTICLE 23 —1. Everyone has the right to work, to free choice of employment, to just and favourable conditions of work and to protection against unemployment.
2. Everyone, without any discrimination, has the right to equal pay for equal work.
3. Everyone who works has the right to just and favourable remuneration insuring for himself and his family an existence worthy of human dignity, and supplemented, if necessary, by other means of social protection.
4. Everyone has the right to form and to join trade unions for the protection of his interests.

ARTICLE 24 —Everyone has the right to rest and leisure, including reasonable limitation of working hours and periodic holidays with pay.

ARTICLE 25 —1. Everyone has the right to a standard of living adequate for the health and well-being of himself and of his family, including food, clothing, housing and medical care and necessary social services, and the right to security in the event of unemployment, sickness, disability, widowhood, old age or other lack of livelihood in circumstances beyond his control.
2. Motherhood and childhood are entitled to special care and assistance. All children, whether born in or out of wedlock, shall enjoy the same social protection.

ARTICLE 26 —1. Everyone has the right to education. Education shall be free, at least in the elementary and fundamental stages. Elementary education shall be compulsory. Technical and professional education shall be made generally available and higher education shall be equally accessible to all on the basis of merit.
2. Education shall be directed to the full development of the human personality and to the strengthening of respect for human rights and fundamental freedoms. It shall promote understanding, tolerance and friendship among all nations, racial or religious groups, and shall further the activities of the United Nations for the maintenance of peace.
3. Parents have a prior right to choose the kind of education that shall be given to their children.

ARTICLE 27 —1. Everyone has the right freely to participate in the cultural life of the community, to enjoy the arts and to share in scientific advancement and its benefits.
2. Everyone has the right to the protection of the moral and material interests resulting from any scientific, literary or artistic production of which he is the author.

ARTICLE 28 —Everyone is entitled to a social and international order in which the rights and freedoms set forth in this Declaration can be fully realized.

ARTICLE 29 —1. Everyone has duties to the community in which alone the free and full development of his personality is possible.
2. In the exercise of his rights and freedoms, everyone shall be subject only to such limitations as are determined by law solely for the purpose of securing due recognition and respect for the rights and freedoms of others and of meeting the just requirements of morality, public order and the general welfare in a democratic society.
3. These rights and freedoms may in no case be exercised contrary to the purposes and principles of the United Nations.

ARTICLE 30 —Nothing in this Declaration may be interpreted as implying for any State, group or person any right to engage in any activity or to perform any act aimed at the destruction of any of the rights and freedoms set forth herein.

UNITED NATIONS

In 1948, a UN committee, led by American Eleanor Roosevelt, created the Universal Declaration of Human Rights. This important document has 30 articles describing the basics rights of all human beings.

- **Education is the key** to many opportunities and resources. Many people can't afford to go to school.
- **Unfair barriers to health services, security, and safety** affect many people worldwide. A lack of insurance, access to care, and unsafe neighborhoods can hugely affect quality of life.

Chapter Six

FACE TO FACE WITH HUMAN NEEDS

There are many chances for people to create social change. Learning about these chances in school has value. However, a face-to-face experience is a direct connection to the problem.

Where does social injustice exist? Right in front of your eyes! There are many instances. For example, say, a person in a grocery store doesn't have enough money to pay for the diapers, milk, and fruit she needs. So, she puts items back to lower the bill. Say a student in your class wants to play hockey but cannot afford the equipment. Or a friend has a bad bruise on his face and says he got punched in the hall. He has bruises a lot. In another example, a person in your neighborhood lost her job and is getting evicted from her apartment. She has no place to go.

Not everyone has the same opportunities in life. It can be hard for some teens to take part in sports, for example. This is especially true of sports that require people to buy a lot of gear.

Examples continue. Say your grandmother's friend stopped taking her medicine because it was too expensive. Increased food costs led to your cousin in college skipping meals. A Jewish temple near your school was spray-painted with hateful words and symbols. Maybe your town has clean water, but the water supply for a town just a few miles away has toxic chemicals in it from a nearby factory. Perhaps an immigrant family fleeing a war zone now lives in an apartment near your neighbor. Many are talking about the family using stereotypes and negative attitudes. Your friend is taking care of his brothers because his parents can't, but he gets a failing grade for not meeting assignment deadlines. Look around, and you will see many human needs.

Chapter Seven

FAIRNESS IN ACTION

Often, it may seem like it's far easier to see injustice, but if you keep your eyes open, you can see fairness in action too. Citizens often need support and services but have trouble finding them. Sometimes local government offices can help people find helpful agencies and experts. Public libraries, government websites, and community leaders can sometimes help remove barriers and make connections with the community. And people just like you can be a driving force for change!

During the COVID-19 pandemic, more government programs paid for school lunch and breakfast. After the programs were cancelled, many more kids couldn't afford to pay for school lunch. Many were forced to run up debt with their schools just to eat. For example, in 2023, Pflugerville school district in Texas had $126,000 worth of unpaid lunch charges owed to the district. Kids who couldn't pay were given a substitute lunch—a cheese sandwich. It was embarrassing for these students.

Brothers John and Maxx Amador decided to lend a helping hand. They started fundraising efforts and used social media and contributions from churches and businesses to pay the lunch debts of all students. They also set up a not-for-profit organization to accomplish this goal.

In another story from California, nine-year-old Ryan Kyote saved his allowance to pay off his classmates' lunch debt. Ryan was inspired to do this when he learned that a five-year-old girl in another district was denied school lunch because she had no money.

It's important to realize that some people have to worry about what they'll have to eat for lunch. Not everyone has the same situation.

Chapter Eight

PROBLEMS SOLVED

Social change depends on identifying problems and solving them. Leaders and other decision-makers, working with active citizens, can sometimes find ways to work against injustice and inequity. Here are a few ways people are trying.

Many times, students and other people without internet access can be seen in business parking lots trying to complete schoolwork using business Wi-Fi. Some may also sit outside libraries or laundromats to do the same thing. Some people must use Wi-Fi connections wherever they can find them, as the basic needs of modern life include digital access. Digital equality has become more of a focus in many public libraries. They may lend digital hot spots and provide other access to digital resources. The federal government has been negotiating with internet providers to offer low-cost internet connections. The Affordable Connectivity Fund will provide some low-income users with a $30 discount on their internet costs.

DACA—Deferred Action for Childhood Arrivals—is a U.S. immigration policy. DACA allows some unauthorized immigrants who were brought to the United States as children to remain in the country long enough to apply for a work permit.

In another issue, many people are working to be sure that laws help guarantee the rights of immigrants to the United States. Some unauthorized immigrants came to the country as children, and some didn't even know they were unauthorized. By law, immigrants have constitutional rights and protections in the areas of civil rights and hate crimes, fair labor, consumer protection, and more.

Immigrants have the right to freedom of speech and religion, the right to be treated fairly, the right to privacy, and the other fundamental rights U.S. citizens enjoy. Everyone in the United States, regardless of citizenship or immigration status, is supposed to be protected under the Civil Rights Act of 1964, which prohibits discrimination because of race, color, religion, sex, or national origin.

Chapter Nine

WHEN CHANGE DOESN'T HAPPEN

History does include examples of progress and social change. But often, people can't solve some problems. There are many barriers in the way. Poverty is one of those barriers, here and around the world.

In 2023, the U.S. Census Bureau reported that nearly 38 million people in the United States were living in poverty. They don't have what they need to meet their basic needs. U.S. poor experience a level of poverty that's worse than those in similar nations. The United States is the richest nation in the world, but its rate of poverty is higher than 25 similar world nations.

In 2023, the U.S. Census Bureau reported the child poverty rate in the United States as 12.4 percent. That means about one in eight children is living in poverty in the United States. Children are the poorest age group in the United States. Children of color, children under five, children of single mothers, and children in the South suffer from the highest poverty rates.

The consequences of childhood poverty last a lifetime. There are barriers to health care and quality education that affect the well-being of children and the adults they become. Food insecurity and poor housing also lead to a poverty cycle. Children growing up in poverty often struggle for educational opportunities that lead to good jobs. Without education and the skills learned through it, they're often employed in low-paying jobs. They carry the burden of poverty along with their children.

Children who grow up in poverty usually face more difficult situations in life, including hunger, illness, and homelessness.

Chapter Ten

GOALS FOR PROGRESS

Social change can be a slow and steady walk up a steep hill. Communities must come together to make change happen. It's important to have goals for what we need to change. Some goals include:

- **Improve schools, especially those serving Black and brown populations, so they deliver quality preparation for life, college, and work. Invest talent, resources, and support to make every student ready for higher education and good-paying jobs.**
- **Make sure there are mentors, role models, tutors, coaches, and caring educators in every school.**
- **Provide the basic elements of survival to all who need them. These include nutrition, clean water, affordable housing, health care, and a living wage.**

Starting or working with a voter registration drive is one way you can work for social justice and help others.

- Find a way to deal with the targeting of and high rates of arrest and imprisonment of Black men.
- Work on solutions for the causes of juvenile crime. These include poverty, family issues, and lack of education.
- Expand diversity in the workplace.
- Eliminate barriers to quality health care and well-being.
- Ensure voting rights, a voice in government, and opportunities for leadership for all people.
- Find solutions for gun violence.
- Find ways to help low-income families with child-care costs, quality, and availability.
- Work for safe housing for low-income families.
- Help people register to vote and improve their access to polling places.

Chapter Eleven

CHECKING IN ON JUSTICE

When fairness fails, you can see it, as can other people in your community. Without fairness, many people won't have the resources they need to thrive. There are many barriers to opportunities and rights.

What does this look like in your community? Perhaps there are families who don't have food, shelter, safety, or heat. Extreme poverty puts their health, security, and growth at great risk. When people don't have enough income, they struggle with basic needs. When people don't earn a living wage, they struggle to survive.

When fairness fails, disadvantages continue. Educational or language barriers affect people's employment. Opportunities to get a good education often depend on quality schools, and it can be hard for poor communities to provide quality schools. So, people can't access their right to fair and equal education. Students in poverty often live with barriers to college, good jobs, and fair income.

Think about the next step when you recognize unfairness in your community. Share your experience and questions with someone you trust, and this can create a way to reflect and understand. You might discover that people are working on solutions to this problem, and they may need allies. This path leads to social change.

Taking your first step in becoming an ally for social justice could be as easy as gathering items for a local food drive. How else could you become a community ally?

Chapter Twelve

MAKING A PLAN FOR ACTION

You might not have thought about taking action before. But when you learn about an injustice in your world, you can choose to be part of the solution. Think about your values and beliefs. You can begin by gathering allies and listening to other perspectives.

Create a goal. An action plan is a list of steps to reach your goal. You can learn from others who have experience with taking this kind of action. Action plans list steps needed to meet a goal. Each step is a task for a team or a person. Leaders keep track of the success of these tasks and adjust the plan if needed.

Deciding to take action can seem like a daunting task. Working as a team, however, can help you find others with similar interests. Teamwork can result in social change!

People can work together to take responsibility for each step. It's important to use creative thinking when you're solving problems. A timeline can be important. One task may often depend on others being complete.

Deciding what resources you need is part of planning. Those resources could be materials, space to work, people, computers, or other items. Work with others to get the resources you need.

Chapter Thirteen

AN ACTION PLAN

As an example, say that one middle school has a goal to create a more united school community. Many differences separate one group from another. A few clubs decide to work together on an action plan to get students to spend time together. They decide to plan an open mic night for acoustic music, garage bands, poetry, and other performances.

Goal: To bring students from different groups together in a shared, positive experience.

Timeline: Six weeks, with volunteers taking responsibilities.

Steps/Tasks: (A few examples)

- Reserve the gym for the date of the open mic.
- Match tasks with talents and interest; reach out to students in different groups.
- Arrange for microphones and seating.
- Talk to kids in bands about sharing one drum set and a public address system.
- Get volunteers to organize a snack table.
- Recruit people from different groups with diverse talents
- Get teacher and parent chaperones and discuss the event with them.
- Sign up volunteers for setup and cleanup.
- Use posters, leaflets, and morning announcements to get the word out.

Evaluate: Have those attending complete an exit card with comments on the experience and their mindset before and after the open mic. Meet and share observations and feedback, photographs, and teacher and parent comments.

Music is a great way to bring people together. You can learn about different music styles, have fun, and make new friends.

Chapter Fourteen

SNEAKERS IN THE SNOW

It's good to stay alert for unfairness and injustice. They're often (but not always) in plain sight. It can be easy for some people not to notice, but you can pay attention. You may notice things that others don't.

What if you see a child wearing thin sneakers in deep, wet snow? What if they have no hat or gloves? It's important to have empathy. How could you help those who don't have the resources to keep warm and dry? Perhaps you have the same problem too.

Many communities have people who are homeless. They may need socks, warm clothes, sleeping bags, and other things. Meanwhile, other people may have coats they never wear. Those people could use their advantages to share and help others in need. Take a step back and think about the ways that you can work for fairness and justice. Think about any tools and resources you might have and put them to work. You might be able to help plan a solution or find allies. You might have transportation or space in which to work. Perhaps you are a good listener or communicator. You may have organizational skills that can help to reach your goals or access to computers and media that can be key advantages in our digital world. You can make the world a better place.

GLOSSARY

apathy: A lack of concern.

collaboration: Working together with others to reach a common goal.

disadvantage: A state or condition that favors someone else.

discrimination: The treating of some people better than others without any fair or proper reason.

empathy: Being aware of and sharing another person's feelings, experiences, and emotions.

evict: To lawfully remove someone from a home.

insurance: A contract by which someone guarantees, for a fee, to pay someone else for the value of property if it is lost or damaged or to pay a specified amount for injury or death.

morale: The mental and emotional condition of an individual or a group with regard to a task or goal to be accomplished.

mosque: A building used for public worship by Muslims.

refugee: An individual who has left their native country and is unwilling or unable to return to it because of persecution or fear of persecution.

satisfaction: The state of being happy with a situation or outcome.

sustainable: Able to continue.

trauma: A serious physical injury.

volunteer: To offer to do something for free.

INDEX